A MOTHER'S GRIEF

Healing from The Loss of a Child.

Tracy Sanford

DEDICATION

To my first-born son, Clinton James King (CJ), you taught me how to be a mama and to love unconditionally with all my heart. I cherish the 33 years we had together.

To my family and friends, you were a lifeline and helped me tremendously on my grief journey. I'm not mentioning names as the list would be long, and I wouldn't want to leave anybody out. Besides, you know who you are; I'm very grateful and blessed for your support, love, and prayers.

To all mamas who've lost their precious child. I hope to make your grief journey a little bit easier. This is a devastating time for you; please be gentle with yourself. I would like to mention my maternal and paternal grandmothers; they both lost babies. I thought about them a lot on my grief journey. Many, many times, I wanted to talk to them about their grief and hear their words of wisdom. I have always admired their strength and strong Christian values.

Contents

ACKNOWLEDGMENTS

I would like to say a special thank you to my family and friends for their love and support during my grief journey. Their support and enthusiasm for my book. I had some great cheerleaders and felt much love. Your ideas, thoughts and encouraging words guided and helped me write and publish this book in less than nine months.

I would like to thank Annie McIndoo for sharing her writing program, which allowed me to heal and honor my son. In the span of three months, it went from an idea to a manuscript.

ABOUT THE AUTHOR

Tracy J Sanford was born in Ventura, California and was raised in Montana mostly on her grandma's property near Thompson Falls. She then raised her two sons' mostly on the same property that she grew up on. She's lived in California, Montana, Utah, Mississippi, Arkansas, Colorado and now lives in Puyallup, Washington.

Tracy lost her oldest son February of 2021. CJ was 33 years old when he died. She struggled to find help due to COVID. She wants to share her grief journey in the hopes of helping another grieving mama. The loss of her son was the hardest experience she ever faced. She will forever grieve for her son but has learned to live with the loss.

INTRODUCTION

I lost my son in February of 2021. My wish is to honor his memory by sharing his story and how I dealt with his death. After my son's passing, I heard many stories about how CJ helped them during a time of struggle in their lives. My hope is to carry on his legacy of helping others by sharing my grief journey with you. This has been the longest and hardest journey I've experienced thus far.

For the longest time, I felt lost. I thought I was going crazy. I had no idea how to help myself. I felt my emotions times ten: anger raged in my body, depression hit me hard, and resentments ate me up inside. I felt like I had fallen into a huge pit of despair. I fumbled in the darkness for a long time, lashing out at those who were trying to help me. I felt like nobody understood what I was feeling; they didn't. They hadn't experienced the loss of a child, so how could they understand? Just understand you are not alone in your grief; others have felt what you are feeling.

Everyone's grief journey is unique. No two people grieve or handle their grief the same way. There's no time limit for grieving. You will forever grieve for your lost loved one, but it does get easier. Not everything I did will work for you, but I've added ideas I discovered while writing this book. There are also ideas for finding help and where to look that guide you in the right direction. You, and only you, can decide who and what will work best for you. I just know one thing: in the early days of my grief, I did not know what kind of help I needed or where to even look. I fumbled along, and God put people in my life who helped me.

Writing this book has been a very healing and life changing experience for me. It has given me back my confidence and self-worth. Sharing this experience is a positive way to help another grieving mama or her family and/or friend.

CJ King "Forever 33"

Chapter 1

The Phone Call

[The Death of a Child

It's like losing your breath and never catching it again.

It's a forever panic attack as your soul is screaming for them.

It's feeling your heart dying as you continue to lose your mind.

Author Unknown.]

I said "Hello" on the phone, and I heard my ex-husband say in a flat voice, "CJ is dead."

My thoughts scream, *'You're wrong. Why are you saying that? What are you saying? Why are you doing this to me? Why would you say anything so horrible? How do you know this? This is not happening.'*

My head is spinning out of control with these thoughts repeating over and over; I hear again, *"CJ is dead."* I asked myself, "How could that be? I just spoke to him."

I could feel my body begin to tremble as I sat there dazed. I could feel myself start to panic. My heart was pounding; it felt like it was going to explode. I finally said, "You're wrong. You don't know what you're talking about."

Then I hear a male voice in the background, "My name is so and so, and I'm a police officer, and ma'am, your son is dead."

I just sat there thinking, *'There's some kind of mistake. You have it wrong. It can't be CJ.'*

I felt this ache in my heart as I put my hand over my breast. It felt like my heart was ripping into two pieces. As I held the phone to my ear with the other hand in a strange voice that sounded far away. I said, "What happened?"

The policeman replies, "Your son died from hypothermia."

I'm thinking, *'CJ hated the cold; he wouldn't be out in the cold long enough to freeze.'* It's all a big mistake. He had just called me on Valentine's Day and said it was cold there. That he had the day off and he was going to stay inside and play video games all day. The policeman continued, "He had COVID, and we believe he was running a fever and didn't realize how cold it was."

Later, the coroner explained to me that because CJ was running a fever, he did not feel the cold. As hypothermia set in, he got sleepy and fell asleep. He didn't feel any physical pain. That was during the Texas Freeze in 2021.

The policeman adds, "He was found near a homeless camp in a grassy area with trees near a ditch of water. Did he live in the homeless camp?"

Later, I discovered CJ had just found out that his best friend since childhood had died. Water had always been calming for CJ. We think he was there in that small slice of nature in the city to grieve for his friend.

I responded, "No."

After a short silence, my mom added, "He had a friend from the homeless camp, and he would take her food and blankets."

My head was still spinning. I kept saying to myself, *This is not real. This is not happening.*

The policeman asked me, "What do you want to do with his body?"

And I'm thinking, *This can't be happening. What I want is for you to take it all back. I want you to bring CJ to me alive and well. I want this to be just a terrible nightmare.*

When I said nothing, Mom said, "He wanted to be cremated."

I just sat there dazed, not knowing what to say or do. I remember thinking he did once say he wanted to be cremated. The policeman says, "Ma'am."

I finally responded, "Yes, please cremate his body and then get him to me as soon as possible."

"Yes, ma'am, and I am very sorry for your loss," responded the police officer. At that point, he said his goodbyes and left.

Then I hear my ex say, "We need to talk. We need to figure out what to do and plan the service." I felt myself withdrawing, cringing at his words. I wanted to shut down and not think or feel.

I finally said, "I can't do this. I can't talk about this right now." I abruptly hung up the phone and handed it back to Mom. Little did I know that phone call would change my life forever. And impacted me emotionally and physically severely for the first few years of my grief journey.

I said, "I can't talk to anybody. You need to tell everyone. I can't handle this. It's too much. Please leave me alone."

Mom says, "Okay, I love you. If you need anything, I'm right here." And she left to go make the phone calls. I got into my bed and covered myself with my blanket, clutching a pillow to my chest, as I cried and sobbed into the pillow.

My whole body was shaking, and I was thinking to myself, *'This isn't happening. It's a big mistake. They all got it wrong. CJ would not be out in the cold long enough to freeze to death. He hated the cold.'*

Then, I decided to call CJ and prove them wrong. I grabbed my phone, and I called him. It didn't ring or go to voicemail. I tried it again, and the same thing happened: nothing; it was dead. So, I decided to text him. I texted him, "CJ, they say you are gone. Please call me to prove them wrong. Please don't leave me like this."

I sat there looking at my phone, crying with no response. My thoughts are racing, and my heart aches. It felt like there was a huge hole in my heart. I laid back in my bed and cried and sobbed. I didn't know my heart could ache so much and that my body could sob and shake so violently.

Later that evening, Mom came into my room, brought some food, and said, "You need to try to eat."

The thought of food made me nauseous. She sat on the edge of my bed and said, "I called everyone."

I didn't know what to say, so all I said was, "Thank you."

She continued, "Everyone is worried about you. They want to help you. They want to tell you that they are sorry this has happened to you, that they love you."

I was feeling very overwhelmed. My emotions were all in turmoil. I just kept thinking I want CJ. I want my baby boy.

I looked at Mom and said, "I can't do this. I can't deal with anyone. I don't want to talk to anybody. Please tell everyone to leave me alone."

And then, after a pause, I said, "Mom, please just leave me alone. I don't want to talk right now."

So, Mom gave me a hug and said, "I love you very much. You are very special to me." Then she reluctantly left me alone, and I laid back down and cried myself to sleep. I spent my days and nights crying myself to sleep long after I got CJ's ashes.

As I lay in bed crying, I kept thinking about when CJ's body was found; he had no identification on him. It took the police a week to identify him and contact me. We suspect he was robbed after he died. According to CJ's roommate, he never left the house without his jacket, his phone, his wallet, his backpack with his laptop, and his motorized bicycle. None of these items were found with CJ, nor were they ever recovered. Whoever took CJ's stuff blocked everyone on his phone list. I would call CJ's number, but I couldn't even hear CJ's voice on his voicemail. I was horrified that someone would steal the belongings of my dead son.

I remember thinking, *'My baby boy is gone. I want my baby back. My sweet baby boy.'*

In my mind, I was seeing CJ as a small boy, not the 33-year-old man he was. Every time I pictured CJ in my head, he was a young boy. He always had a smile on his face, my blond-haired, blue-eyed, perfect little boy. From the time he was small, he gave the best hugs. He was such a lover boy. CJ was such a happy baby, always laughing.

I wanted CJ so much. I could hardly wait to be a mama. When CJ was three or four months old, I started holding him with his ear close to my mouth, and I would whisper in his ear. I would say, "I love you. You are my sweet baby boy. You are so precious to me". He would smile and coo. He loved that; CJ started leaning his ear close to my mouth, wanting me to whisper in his ear. That quickly became a private moment that I will always cherish in my heart. It was the first image of CJ I pictured in my head when I learned CJ was gone.

Tracy whispering in CJ's ear

[Clearly, we grieve the person we lost.

What many don't understand is that is only part of it.

We grieve what we had and all that we shared.

We grieve all the important things that they have missed and will miss.

We grieve the future we were supposed to have together.

This list goes on. Grief is complicated.

Joni Grieftolife.com]

A week before I found out about CJ, I had a dream about this sweet lady who was bedridden that I had met the year before. We talked about crocheting and our families. She showed me the things she had been making. I visited her in the mornings and evenings for about a week in her bedroom. She died about seven weeks before CJ did. In my dream, we talked once again about crocheting and about our families. I would wake up and then go back to sleep and pick up the dream where we last left off. I remember waking up the next morning thinking that was an odd dream. I now realize that she sat with me in my dreams the night CJ became an angel.

[This is a thing many people outside your grief cannot understand:

That you have not simply lost one person at one point in time.

You have lost their presence in every aspect of your life.

Your future has changed, as well as your "now."

Megan Devine - @refuge in grief.]

Chapter 2

The Emotional Rollercoaster

[I don't know what grief will look like tomorrow. But I will face it.

I'll feel it. As your memory washes over me. One day at a time. One wave at a time.

For such a love, Grief is the price of admission. The cost of the human condition.

So, I'll pay for it over and over again until I see you again. The love was worth it.

Liz Newman]

I was in total denial until I got CJ's ashes. I kept trying to call him, only to be heartbroken when I got nothing on the other end. I would text CJ, "Please call me. Please text me. Come home. CJ, I need you. CJ, I want your back. CJ, just please answer me."

Every time my phone rang, or I got a text message, I was disappointed that it wasn't from CJ. I kept thinking he would walk through that door and wrap his arms around me and say, "It's okay, Mom. I'm here." But he never did. By denying the loss, it gave me time to slowly absorb what had happened. It numbed me from the intensity of the loss.

Tracy Sanford (a message I posted on CJ's Facebook page).]

I was devastated when I first held CJ's ashes in my arms; tears soaked my face. I thought, "This isn't real. This is a bad dream. This is not happening. You can't be gone."

I wanted to scream these words as I hugged CJ's ashes close to my heart. I spent the next few weeks with CJ's ashes held close, crying into my pillow until I fell into an exhausted sleep. I would say, "God, please give me CJ back. I need him here with me. Please don't take him away."

My thoughts then changed to "God, please let me die in my sleep, too. If you won't bring CJ back to me, I don't want to live. I can't live without CJ. Please don't make me. You know, I won't commit suicide because it's a mortal sin. So, God, please just take me; put me out of my misery. I can't do this anymore."

I would cry that over and over, night after night.

I became very suicidal. My counselor said I was passive-suicidal. I wanted to die, but I hadn't made any plans to act on it. I wanted to go to sleep and not wake up. I would text and message my family and friends, crying about how much I hurt and that I didn't want to live. That I wanted to die in my sleep. I would continue with I won't kill myself. I don't want to go to hell. Then, when they were all in bed, I would call a suicide hotline and talk to them for hours. Oftentimes, nobody knew what to say or do to help me. As soon as it would get dark out-side, the grief became overwhelming and unbearable.

[Grief is like a snowflake… sometimes, it comes one flake at a time,

other times, it comes like a blizzard. It melts away, but it always comes back.

Just as each snowflake is unique, each person experiences grief in their own unique way.

Myfamandme.com]

One morning, I was on the verge of ending my life. I found myself in the emergency room. It was taking a long time to be seen, so I left without seeing the doc. I had told them I was suicidal when I checked in. The next thing I knew, a police offi-cer called me and said he would like to take me to the hospital. They picked me up at a friend's house, and they were very nice and helpful. I stayed in the hospital for three days, where they kept me safe.

Less than a month later, I was back at the hospital; I was put on medication that helped stabilize my mood. I was still passive-suicidal, but my mood swings were not quite so dra-matic. I took the meds for over two years. Then, slowly, with the help of my doctors, I stopped taking the antidepressants. Depression is not easy or well-defined. It can be messy and difficult. I isolated myself from others to fully cope with my grief. I often felt foggy, heavy, and confused. I ended up need-ing professional help.

I was angry at everyone, and everything, any little thing

would set me off. I knocked over a pitcher of tea in the fridge and I started yelling and screaming. I went to grab a towel to clean it up and before I got the towel, I grabbed a bunch of bananas and threw them up against the wall. I went into my bedroom and slammed the door and cried myself to sleep leaving mom to clean up my mess.

Another time, I got mad at my laptop because it wasn't working again. I had a friend try to fix it with no luck. I remember raising the laptop over my head and yelling, "CJ, it's your fault. You were supposed to fix it for me, and now you are dead and can't fix it. It's not fair. I'm mad at you. I'm mad at God."

And then I slammed the laptop to the floor, and it broke into several pieces. I crawled into bed, leaving the smashed laptop on the floor, and cried myself to sleep. I had a very short fuse. I felt like a big, massive ball of anger. I had no control over my feelings or emotions. I had horrible mood swings. Any little thing could and would set me off, and once I lost control, I didn't know what to do, so I would go into my room and lock it, bury my head under my blankets, and cry myself into an exhausted sleep.

As the denial faded, my emotions came to the surface. I became extremely angry, which was another way of hiding my intense emotions from the pain and anguish of losing CJ. The anger was directed at someone, an object, or even at situations. In the moment of rage, I did not realize my anger was directed at the wrong target.

I had a lot of resentments towards my family. It took me almost two years to work through them. I avoided many family members. I could not get over my anger at some of their actions. I let my resentments build and grow into rage. Anger will also mask itself with emotions of resentment and bitterness. You blame others for the intense feelings you cannot control.

For the first twenty months, I felt like I was stuck in my grief. I had no control over how I was feeling. My emotions were dark and cold. I was filled with a rage that felt like it might explode like a bomb. I wished I was dead. I lashed out at everyone and every little thing. That was my mental state.

When I started GriefShare, I went into the group thinking, this is my last shot at trying to come back from the pit of grief. I threw myself into the program. I questioned everything and everyone in the program. I paid attention to the videos. I shared my thoughts and feelings about each session. I did the homework faithfully. I was brutally honest. Two amazing ladies ran the program. I talked to them. They checked on me throughout the week, and they prayed for me. Their kindness and support helped me to work through my grief and heal.

I had a lot of people praying for me. One of the group leaders had lost a son many years ago, so I paid close attention to her when she spoke. My grandma was a Pentecostal preacher, so I believed in God and studied the Bible. One night in the group, they discussed how God will not forgive you until you forgive others. In AA, I learned you have to forgive others for their wrongdoings if you want to overcome your resentment. I started thinking about that. I had to let go of my resentments because the person I was angry with did the best they could in that situation at that time; nobody is perfect. We all make mistakes.

I started reaching out to my family and apologizing for my initial silence, my anger, and my verbal lash outs. Everyone was very forgiving and said that they understood I was going through a horrible time. The biggest thing I learned in Grief-Share was that grief is unique. Nobody has the same grief journey. Grief is very personal. Grief is messy. There is no time limit. There is no right or wrong way to grieve, but you need to feel the emotions to get through the grief. Numbing yourself to the pain only prolongs the grief process. You must feel the grief to heal.

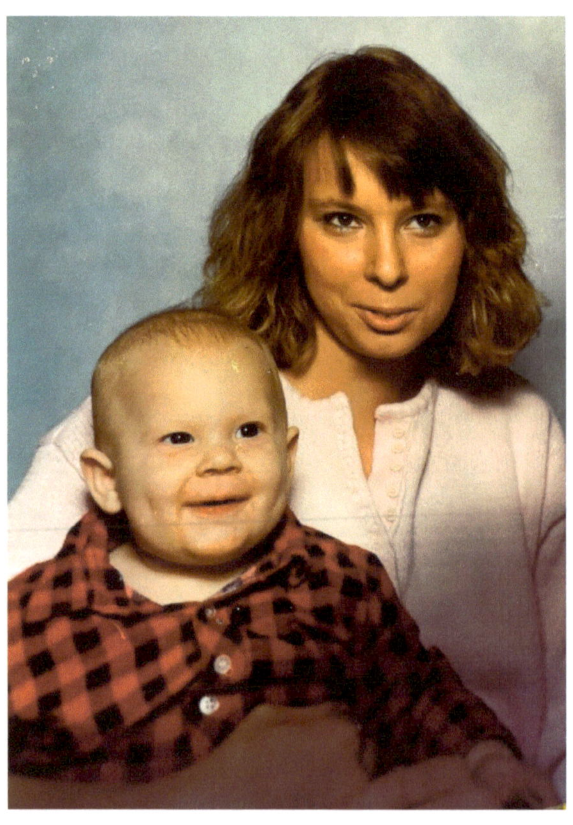

Tracy & CJ

I never really accepted CJ's death until I was going to Grief Share, which was twenty months after he was gone. Before that, I begged God to give me back CJ or for Him to take my life. I couldn't imagine living my life without CJ. I was more focused on the loss, what was taken from me. I learned I needed to focus on the good. That I had 33 amazing years with my son. I began cherishing my memories. I started smiling along with the tears. That did not magically make me happy. It just meant I had accepted the loss. I am now learning to live without my son. I even have happy moments. I'll forever have sad days. I'll always miss him. The hole in my heart will always be there.

[It's okay if you thought you were over it, but it hits you all over again.

It's okay to fall apart even after you thought you had it under control. You are not weak.

Healing is messy. There is no timeline for healing.]

Still, to this day, one of my first thoughts in the mornings is that CJ is gone. Sometimes, it still makes me sad, and sometimes, I just start talking to CJ and tell him how much I love and miss him, and I always will. I know he's there, but I just don't see him. I talk to CJ all day long. This is my new normal. I will never look at my youngest son, grandbabies, or family and friends the same way again. Life is so short. Nothing is guaranteed in this life. I will always hug them a little bit tighter and a little bit longer. Grief is an unbearable emotion to handle all at once. Grieve your way. Many will try to help you. They mean well. Most won't understand the depth of your grief. They have not experienced a loss like you have.

There is no loss worse than that of a child. Once it happens, you are a member of a club nobody wants to belong to. We are often misunderstood and forgotten, and when we come out on the other side, we are stronger and better from surviving the loss. Grief will always be a part of our lives.

The first year of CJ's death, I was numb. It's mostly a blur. I don't remember things I said or did. I don't remember what others said to me. I have bits and pieces of my memory. The second year really hit me, and I felt everything times ten; all the pain and emotions were right on the surface. My grief was overwhelming and overpowering. If I wanted to come out on the other side of this grief, I needed to feel the pain. I needed to fully experience every painful stage of grief and feel all those emotions, and I did. And the third year was my healing year. I started living again. I left my comfort zone—which was my bedroom—and I started a new hobby with many possibilities.

I went on adventures and reached out to old friends. As I head into the fourth year of CJ's death, I want to help others. That's why I'm writing this book. If I can help one person that makes it all worthwhile.

Chapter 3

The Demons

Tracy Sanford (a message to CJ on Facebook)]

Within a few days of hearing about the death of my son, I started seeing shadows out of the corner of my eyes; I would turn and see nothing. It was very unnerving. I felt like someone was in the room watching me. A week later, I saw them for the first time. I was in my room on my bed, curled up in a ball. They were sitting in my doorway, watching me. There were only two or three of them that night. As time went by, the demons grew in numbers until there were 12 or 14 demons in total. At first, I only saw them in my bedroom. Then, as they grew in numbers, so did the places I saw them until they were always visible to me everywhere I went. The closest they ever got was about two feet.

They resembled coyotes, but they were broader and bigger. They were hunched back, giving them a massive round shape. Their fur was long and black, thick and tangled. It stood straight out wildly, making them look even bigger. Their heads were huge but had the shape of a coyote. They had a long, narrow black nose. The ears resembled a German shepherd, long and pointy, and they stood straight up with lots of hair sticking out everywhere.

Their mouths were always open, with their pinkish-red tongues hanging almost to the floor. They had two rows of ugly, yellow, long, pointy teeth. It seemed like they couldn't close their mouths around their teeth and tongue. Their eyes seemed small on their faces. Their pupils were black and empty; you could get lost in the darkness of their black beady eyes. The whites of their eyes were bloodshot, mostly red. Their paws were massive, resembling a puppy that hadn't grown into his big paws yet. The claws were long and black and had an almost hook-like shape to them.

I verbalized to many people, many times, that I was seeing demons, that they were in my room watching me all night, and then eventually, I was seeing them during the day, everywhere I went. I would say they scare me. I can't sleep at night, and they are always watching me. I would tell the demons to go away and to leave me alone. I would wish them away. I prayed to God, please take them away. Later, many people said that they thought I meant it figuratively. I wondered why nobody ever did anything to help me.

About ten months after CJ passed away, I was out of town; our hotel was near a busy street. I decided to enjoy the sunshine and go for a walk. I thought perhaps I would find a fun store to shop at. I walked by this house with a sign in the yard that read 'Psychic.' A friend of mine had told me a few weeks earlier that her husband went to a psychic, and she was spot on about him.

We also talked about how a psychic might help to give me some peace about CJ's passing. I kept on walking past the house. I was nervous about what I might find out. Didn't know if I was ready to venture into the unknown or if this person was a true professional. Later that morning, I walked back by the house. I thought, "What the hell?" When I walked through the door, there were shelves and tables filled with rocks and crystals she had for sale. I was looking around, and she was making small talk with me. Then, out of nowhere, she said, "Why are you so sad"? I told her my son had recently died.

Then she asked, "Are you a believer?"

I told her I wasn't sure that I had several family members who believed and sought their fortune many times. She asked, "Do you want to know your fortune?"

I said, "Maybe."

Then, her next question caught me by surprise. She said, "Do you see them? Can you see the black creatures following you? And there's more outside waiting." I had not said anything to her about them. I had not looked at them. I had not even acknowledged them.

I told her, "Yes, they have been following me since my son died." We both agreed that they were scary.

Then she said she could banish them for me, and so told me how much it would cost. I literally started crying and said, "I don't have that kind of money".

She continued, "That is the only way to get rid of them'.

I told her, "No, thank you," and started out the door. I was very disappointed.

She then says, "Wait a minute." As she's talking to me, she pulls out a baggie with tiny shards of crystals.

She continues, "Place a small handful of these in your bath water along with Epsom salt and baking soda, light white candles, and with good thoughts, with the demons away."

Then she also gave me a six-inch white pillar candle and said, "Light it every Sunday for six consecutive weeks and repeat the same prayer."

I thanked her, and I left with a little bit of hope in my heart. I went home and followed her instructions to the letter. Unfortunately, the demons were still following me. They were still watching me. I was very discouraged and didn't think they would ever go away.

[It's 2:22 am. Sleep is a long way off.

I miss you, CJ…

Why did you leave me???

Tracy Sanford (a message to CJ on Facebook)]

One night, I was messaging a longtime friend from Montana. I told her I was sitting on my bed with a blanket wrapped around me. I was scared that the demons were watching me and that there were so many in my room, in my bathroom, and in the doorway. There were so many that they couldn't all fit in my room. I described them to her, saying that they were always around and that the number of them kept growing. I told her about the psychic the month before. She told me that her sister-in-law lived close to me, that she was a preacher, and had been for years. That she really trusted her, and I could too.

She said she would reach out to her, tell her my story, give her my phone number, and maybe she could help me. She gave me hope that night.

A few days later, the preacher called me. She said she could help me if I was interested. We talked for a while. She was very kind and sympathetic. She prayed with me. She told me to read my Bible daily. I told her that I had just started reading my Bible again, that I had been very angry with God for taking my son, and that I had been yelling at God, and she said that it was okay because God could handle it. She said to sleep with my Bible in my bed. Listen to this app (PRAY.COM) on my phone when I go to bed for the night. It recited Bible verses. The preacher said she wanted to check into how to best help me. The demons continued to follow me.

She called me a few days later and said she would like to do a prayer to cast them away. After the prayer, she told me to go home and read specific verses from the Bible, continue listening to the verses, and sleep with my Bible. The demons were never in my car, so I wasn't sure if it had worked yet or not. I got home, and there were no demons following me and none in my room. I never saw them again after that day. I still sleep with my Bible.

Chapter 4

The Memorial

[Losing a child makes you feel like you're being torn apart from the inside out.

inside out.

Author unknown]

My ex kept bugging me about a memorial service for CJ, wanting us to plan it and attend the service together. I would say, "I'm not ready." I couldn't even imagine attending one, let alone planning one. I finally told him to do what he wanted with whoever he wanted and to please leave me out of it. He wanted to know if I was going to have one. I told him no; it was too sad. I felt that way for months. My counselor suggested I have the memorial when I was ready. There's nothing written in stone stating when you should have one. And if I choose to do so, I don't have to have one at all.

The summer after CJ passed, I talked to my family, and we all wanted to get together and do something in remembrance of CJ. After considerable thought, I decided to create a memorial in our hometown in Montana. That's where so many years of our lives were spent together. My kids spent most of their childhood in Sanders County; the mountains, lakes, rivers, and creeks were their playground. We hiked the mountains and trails and swam every body of water we could get to. We camped in many of the parks. We fished, hunted, and picked mushrooms and berries. Many happy memories.

The second weekend in June, four months after CJ's death I was finally ready. I made a bed in the back of my station wagon and loaded a few items to camp in my car in the woods with. Windows rolled down, music blaring, I set off to Thompson Falls in search of the perfect spot for the memorial. CJ was riding a shotgun in his urn.

As I drove into Montana, the memories washed over me, and I started crying. My first stop was the Thompson Falls Dam, my very favorite spot in Montana. I spent my entire life going and hanging out on that little island next to the dam. The island has changed over the years. As a child, I could roam the entire island freely. Climbing on the rocks, walking on and around the bridges, playing in the cave. You could then drive over the bridge onto the island. Now you can only walk out there, plus there are fences everywhere limiting where you can go. It was bittersweet walking the island. So many memories.

I continued going to our different swimming holes. I would wander around, put my feet in the water, and talk to CJ. I would ask, "Where do I want to do this? What kind of memorial should I do? How do I honor your life?" I talked to CJ, reminiscing about some of my favorite memories. Asking him if he remembered this or that. I cried. I laughed. I yelled. I screamed at the wind. It gave me some comfort. An onlooker would have thought I had lost my mind.

My last stop was Beaver Creek. I parked in the primitive camp area and walked down to the water. I was about to put my feet in the water, and as I looked down, I found my first heart-shaped rock of the day. I picked it up and held it close to my heart and looked up into the sky and said, "thank you, CJ."

I knew CJ was there with me and that was comforting.

I was crying as I started walking upstream. I had taken maybe a dozen steps when I found my second heart-shaped rock. As I picked it up, I looked at the sky and said, "WOW, thank you, son. You must realize my struggle today." With a heart-shaped rock in each hand, I continued upstream. Within a few minutes, I found my third heart-shaped rock. I got very excited. I shouted, "This is the spot. We found it. CJ, thank you for the third heart-shaped rock. Three has always been my favorite number. CJ died at 33 years old, so I now associate the number three with CJ, especially if I see 33. When I see 33 on my alarm clock, I always think of CJ and say to him, "You must be thinking about me. I love you so much, son."

With all three heart shaped rocks in my hands. I said, "okay CJ, we found the spot, but where do we put the Cross? It will get washed away down here by the water."

I started walking along the bank. As I went upstream, I saw a tiny, star-shaped pink flower. I said, "It's your favorite color." Up the path, I could see the second star-shaped pink flower. I walked toward the flower, thinking this was the way to go. I then spotted the third star-shaped pink flower. I looked up, seeing the water, and then I slowly turned around in a few circles, looking at the grassy banks, the trees, and the mountains in the distance. I could hear birds and squirrels over the sound of the creek flowing gently downstream. The mountain air smelled fresh and crisp. I thought this was the perfect spot; it was so beautiful and peaceful.

Up the path toward a small clearing, I saw a small purple flower. I walked toward it, thinking about a recent conversation where CJ expressed how much he liked purple. As I stood there with the flower at my feet, I spotted the second purple flower up ahead. The third flower stood a short distance away. I said, "Okay, we have three sets of three." This is perfect. In the clearing, there were wildflowers everywhere, with bees, butterflies, and dragonflies hovering over the flowers. There was a big, beautiful bush right where two creeks merged into one bigger creek. I thought there was enough room for everyone to gather, and there was even an access road so you could drive up to the clearing. I got so excited. Yelling, "CJ, we found the spot. This is where I can come to visit with you. I will put your Cross and memorial bench right here. Unfortunately, the Forest Service would not allow me to leave the bench there, but I was able to leave the Cross there.

That night, I camped up Beaver Creek in the primitive campground. I built myself a small fire. As I listened to nature's late-night song, I gazed at the wide-open sky with so many stars shining brightly around an almost full moon. I slept in the back of my station wagon with the sunroof and the back hatch door open. I woke up early to a beautiful sunrise. I walked down to the water and washed my face. As I started toward my car, I looked around and smiled.

[I am grateful for your life… even as I mourn your death.

I laugh at the memories… even as I cry for those not made.

I recognize the beauty in life… even as I experience its ugliness.

I embrace hope and joy… even as my heart breaks.

I live… even as I grieve.

all-greatquotes.com]

Happy with my choice for the memorial I packed my car for the trip home. I talked to CJ planning the memorial as I drove down the mountain. I clocked the mileage for directions to get to the memorial site; it was exactly 3.3 miles to the main road. There were the threes again.

I was halfway home when I started getting sleepy and very hungry. I spotted this little bar and thought, I love bar hamburgers. I went inside and ordered. The bartender commented on my necklaces. I told her they were my memorial necklaces for my son, who had passed away four months earlier.

I told her the moon read, "I love you to the moon and back," with a heart hanging from the tip that had "son" engraved on it with my son's ashes inside. I took off the necklace with a crystal and told her to hold it up to the light, and you could just see a picture of my son. She thought that was very cool. She gave me a hug and said, "I'm sorry for your loss." I shed a few tears at her kindness. I told her about going to Montana and camping for the weekend and how I found the perfect spot for the memorial. I told her about talking to CJ and finding the rocks and the flowers. She said that was a beautiful story. The bartender kept asking me questions, so I shared my story.

I was getting ready to leave when she asked me to hang on for a minute. She needed to go out to her car. I thought she wanted me to keep an eye on the bar while she was gone, so I sat back down. She comes back in with a wooden plaque that has a clip on it to hang a picture. Across the bottom was written, I love you to the moon and back. It had a moon and some stars painted on it. She handed it to me and said, "I bought this to put a photo of my son in. I tell him I love him to the moon and back all the time, but I think you should have this for a photo of your son."

I hugged her, thanked her for kindness for a lost mama and that I would put it in CJ's Memorial Showcase. I cried all the way to the car and for many miles down the road. It was so sweet, the kindness a stranger showed towards me.

During the weekend of CJ's memorial, I camped at CJ's memorial site in the primitive campground with two of CJ's cousins and one of his close, longtime friends. They all grew up together and called CJ their brother. We couldn't have a fire because the fire danger was so high. I had a big citronella candle to burn, so we put that in the fire pit and lit it. CJ sat in a chair in our circle in his urn. We talked about CJ and shared stories. I heard many stories for the first time about the crazy and sometimes dangerous adventures they had while growing up, and this brought me closer to my son. The kids had many times jumped a train to get to a nearby town where they hung out and swam. Then, they would jump on another train to get home. I was shocked at the stories and wondered how they were still in one piece.

The day before the service, we piled into one car with CJ in his urn in the middle back seat buckled in. We went to all of CJ's favorite spots and our favorite swimming holes. One of the kids would carry CJ in his urn. Everywhere we went, we took turns releasing a handful of CJ's ashes into the wind as we stood on the water's edge, the ashes landing in the water. We continued sharing stories, laughing and crying. At one point during the day, my cousin, who I grew up with, joined us on our trip down memory lane.

At every stop, I put my feet in the water and found a rock to take home. I took pictures of the beautiful scenery. It was a very healing day. My heart was full of the love I had for CJ.

On the morning of CJ's memorial, we put up signs with balloons guiding everyone to the memorial site. I had pictures and poems sitting on CJ's memorial bench with three vases of flowers in front. Next to the bench was CJ's Cross, which had his name carved on it, and painted rocks circled the cross. I had asked everyone to bring a painted rock to place around the Cross. There were so many cool rocks, a pizza one, a ladybug, an eraser, a big rainbow. Some had smiley faces, hearts, flowers, and messages. There were so many shapes and sizes and so many colors. There was a rock wrapped in wire. There was even one with a pick of CJ on it.

CJ's memorial up Beaver Creek in Trout Creek, Mt.

Many asked me about the dress code. At first, I wanted everyone to dress up because CJ liked to dress nicely in a tie and dress shirt. Then, after some thought, I told everyone to dress for CJ their way. Some showed up wearing CJ's favorite color, a T-shirt with CJ's favorite band, or a character he liked. Some were paired with shorts or jeans. Some wore dresses, and there was even someone with a tie and a dress shirt. I wore a black skirt with a purple top. It was interesting to see how everyone dressed for CJ.

I decided against a preacher since all the ones that we knew were long gone, so I asked my mom to do an opening prayer, and then my dad said the closing prayer. In between the prayers, I encouraged everyone to come forward and share a favorite story they had about CJ. I had a big crystal vase with ivy painted on it. I also had three different colors of sand close to the vase with a scoop nearby. I asked everyone to grab a scoop of sand after they shared their story and pour it into the vase. The vase was filled with layers of sand as the love was shared. In the end, I had a beautiful vase with layers of sand representing a loving memory of CJ in different colors. The vase sits in CJ's memorial showcase, reminding me of every story told that day.

The service seemed almost magical, with butterflies everywhere. They kept landing on everyone like they were giving kisses and loving touches of comfort. There was even a hummingbird that flew around the three bouquets of flowers in front of CJ's bench. After the service, many came up to me and said, "What a beautiful service. It was so magical with all the butterflies and the loving stories shared by all. There was so much love there that day, and it wrapped its arms around everyone. Nobody left unaffected by the day; my heart healed a bit from that experience. I was very glad I waited until I was ready to have CJ's memorial.

[I have heard it said that the greatest loss a human being can experience is the loss of a child.

This is true. It doesn't just change you. It demolishes you.

The rest of life is spent on another level.

Gloria Vanderbilt]

[5. photo of CJ, Brandon and I].   (CJ, Brandon and I. we had all just gotten new glasses.)

Chapter 5

Family and Friends

[I believe the hardest part of healing after you lose someone you love,

It is to recover the "you" that went away with "them."

Kelly's Treehouse]

Everyone was very supportive of my wishes. They respected my desire to be left alone. I was very grateful. Many stepped up, so I didn't have to worry about anything. My mom told everyone about CJ's passing and kept everyone informed about how I was doing. My ex had CJ cremated. One of my brothers went to CJ's home in Austin, Texas, and packed his personal items, donated some of his things, and then mailed the boxes to me. He also talked to the investigating officer and even went to the area where CJ was found. My cousin got CJ's ashes from my ex and took them to my other brother, who brought them to me. He also had a beautiful urn shipped to my house.

I was so angry and full of resentment towards everyone. I thought for the longest time that if others had done things differently, CJ might still be alive. It took me a long time to realize that everyone had their own lives to live, and CJ could have reached out to them as easily as they could have to him.

I would often get angry alone by my thoughts. My brain would work overtime, rehashing old drama and hurts. The rage would grow inside of me until I lashed out at loved ones. I would get angry and yell at them and say hurtful mean things. I did not know how to get my anger out. I often didn't even know why I was angry.

With guidance, I started yelling into my pillow, punching and hitting it. I would scream as loud as I could. One night, my neighbor knocked on my door and asked if I was okay and if he could hear me screaming. I would also scream in the car. I would yell and cuss at CJ, at God, at the driver in front of me, or some unknowing loved one.

I even resented the fact that nobody sent CJ flowers after he died. I was hurt. I only got a handful of sympathy cards. I felt like nobody cared enough to acknowledge CJ's death or my grief. I was very appreciative of the cards I got. It took me a long time to understand that people don't bring food over or send flowers or sympathy cards anymore. It's a forgotten tradition.

I didn't understand what I was feeling or how to control my emotions, so it was unfair of me to think and expect everyone else to understand. They did the best they could to try to help me. I felt like I needed so much help but did not know who to ask, where to go, or even what type of help I needed. I just felt so out of control and that my emotions were grossly intensified.

Thankfully, my family all stood by my side. They let me lash out at them for as long as I needed. Everyone was very forgiving and understanding when I made amends with each of them.

On top of my grief, which added to the intensity of my emotions, I was experiencing horrible insomnia. Many nights, I didn't sleep at all, or I would only sleep a few hours total for the night. Nightmares interrupted what little sleep I did get. One night, I dreamed about CJ freezing. I could feel his body getting cold. It was like I was experiencing his death. It left me with a chill for days, and journaling and talking to my counselor finally helped me to accept the way he died.

I would text and message my friends from far away at all hours of the night, pouring out my heart, my hurts, my sadness, my depression, my anxiety, everything I could not verbalize.

I got so much support and love. Many had no idea how close I was to the edge, that their kind words were my saving grace, and that they helped me through a moment of hell, a moment of total despair. I often felt like I was a Debbie Downer, that I was bothering others with my grief. I felt I was imposing on their lives with my desperate struggle to get out of the deep hole. I would try not to reach out and be bothersome. Then, I would be drowning in my grief, and I would finally send out a lifeline. Sometimes, they would not answer right away, so I would often text someone else. I often got a text the next morning saying that they had just received my message. Asking what they could do to help me, saying that they cared and that they were praying for me. I truly believe those late-night messages saved my life. I will forever be grateful to all those who took the time out of their lives to help me.

To make matters worse, my health issues got worse. All my health issues intensified, and many more appeared. It took an extra-long time to resolve them. I let my healthcare team know about my loss, which they said was important information to have for them to treat me properly.

A huge struggle I had was being alone in my bed late at night. I've always liked being single until I was lost in my grief. I had a few friends who came over on some of my darkest nights and held me while I cried myself to sleep. So many people helped me in little ways that kept blindly pushing me forward.

One friend was always a phone call away, standing on the sideline supporting me. No matter what I was doing, I would scream at him, tell him he didn't understand what I was feeling, that he didn't care. I would rant and rave. I would go off on him for the strangest reasons. He would quietly leave me alone. I never saw his tears or how helpless he felt as he looked away. As he took a step back one day, he said, "I will be happy when you get back to your old self."

I screamed." She died with CJ. Now I don't know who I am."

[Doing this life without you has changed me. I'm just not the same person anymore.

How could I be? One thing that will never change, though, is the love I hold in my heart for you.

Nothing, including any amount of time that goes by, could change that.

Joni Roberts]

He said the saddest thing that he ever saw was me sitting on the bed; all huddled up crying in the hospital emergency room when he and Mom had to leave me alone. He was always there for me; to hold my hand, give me a hug, give me a shoulder to cry on, to be my verbal punching bag. I tested our friendship many times. He never turned his back on me.

Mom also endured many of my outbursts and fits of rage. She felt helpless watching me from the doorway. Mom was always there for me. She made sure I ate. She had to take care of the house and yard because I didn't care about anything. Her constant prayers, along with so many other prayers for me, were my saving grace.

My dad lives a few states over from me. He never pushed me to talk on the phone. He would text his love and support for me. My dad and stepmom sent me cards with loving support. My stepmom wrote a grief poem on some beautiful paper that she found not long after her mother passed. She said it helped her and thought it might help me. Now, I'm sharing it with you in the hopes that it will help you a little:

["We thought of you with love today,

But that is nothing new.

And the days before that, too.

We think of you in silence.

We often speak your name.

Now, all we have is memories.

And your picture in a frame.

Your memory is our keepsake,

With which we'll never part.

I had another friend, several states over, who I would message late at night. I would pour out my heart to her. Whatever was in my head, sometimes it was a rambling mess. She would come back with great words of wisdom. Most of the time, I felt better after talking to her. One night, I thanked her for her great support and how much it meant to me. Her reply touched me to the center of my soul. She said, "I had no idea what to say. I have not experienced a loss like yours. I truly believe CJ is guiding me on what to say to help you." I will forever be grateful for her late-night chats. She talked, and I was off the edge many times. She also made phone calls trying to get me some help in my area.

I had another friend who I texted late at night. Luckily, he was an insomniac. Years before, he lost his son at an early age. I would literally verbally vomit my emotions and thoughts. He could come back and basically repeat what I said, and it made sense, and it helped. He also shared how he felt in the early days of his loss. I would say, yes, that's me. Then, he would share how he handled it, whether it was the right solution or not. He heard all my ugly thoughts and feelings. Thankfully, he didn't judge me.

CJ kissing his baby brother

My cousin grew up with my boys, and quite often, she would come with us on our adventures. Her brother went with us too when he was visiting our family. She was the only one I talked to on the phone in the early days of my grief. She still calls me and checks on me. She always reaches out to me on Valentine's Day, the Anniversary of CJ's death day, his birthday, Mother's Day, Thanksgiving, and Christmas. She's a bright spot on the hard days. As a result of CJ's death, my cousin and I have grown closer together, and we stay in touch more. For that, I am truly grateful.

It took me a long time before I could finally accept the fact that CJ was gone. I kept telling CJ to come back to me. I would beg God to send him back, and then I would get angry with God when he didn't. I would post on CJ's Facebook page.

CJ, come back to me. I need a CJ hug. For the longest time, all my letters to CJ have started with CJ. Please come back. I need you. I miss you. I love you. I can't do life without you. Again, "GriefShare" helped me to move past those thoughts. I don't beg him to come back anymore, but I still tell him how much I love him, and I miss him.

Unfortunately, not everyone knows how to help you in your grief journey. I had a friend that I ran into a few months into my grief. She told me she didn't know what to say to me, so she avoided me. That hurt a lot. Unfortunately, we are no longer friends, her choice. People would casually say, you should be doing better now. CJ has been gone a long time, or they would ask, why aren't you over those feelings by now? Luckily for me, those were just a few. Those comments came from people on my grief groups online, not from my friends and family. They have been and still are very supportive.

Here's a great strategy to reach out to those close to you;

Write a grief letter to your family and friends. Explain your feelings and struggles. Let them know what to do and what not to do. Tell them where you need help, for instance, with housework, yard work, babysitting, or if they could bring you a covered dish for dinner once a week, or give you a hug or just sit with you while you cry, to listen while you verbally vomit, or for them to give you space, but remind them to please not forget about you. Remember, most don't truly understand the depth of your grief and have no idea how to help you, but they want to.

[My child died, and now I don't know who I am…

Silentgriefsupport.com]

CHAPTER 6

One Day at a Time

[Imagine living with a scream inside you. And this scream is yours. And no one else hears it…

That. Is. Grief.

Widow's Hope]

"Just for today, I will try to live through this day only, and not tackle my whole life's problem at once. "That is an AA, "just for today's quote." In the early days of my grief, I didn't do much. In fact, I didn't even get out of bed even after I started getting out of bed. I did not want to do anything. I didn't have the energy to do household chores or attempt to attend to my responsibilities. It quickly built up and became overwhelming, making it even harder to tackle any of it, which added another element to my grief.

I spent most of my life in and out of AA. One thing I learned was to take it one day at a time. Sometimes, you need to take it one hour at a time and even one minute at a time. That helped me tremendously in my grief journey. I would self-talk; don't think about it in terms of the rest of your life. I needed to quit thinking I couldn't live the rest of my life without CJ. I decided I would live just for today without CJ. I will get through today. Tomorrow is another day, another 24 hours. Tomorrow, I can decide what to do next. Just hang on until tomorrow.

Emotionally, that was all I could handle at the time. For a long time, in my grief, making any type of decision was overwhelming. There's that word again overwhelming. Most everything in grief is overwhelming. If I didn't have to make the decision right away, I would tell myself, "Wait 'till tomorrow, just get through today. It will still be there tomorrow."

When I was close to following CJ, I didn't think I could move on in my grief; I thought about ending my life the same way CJ did so I would be sure to see him in the afterlife. I self-talked myself to take it one day at a time. That, I would stick around for the next 24 hours. I told myself, you don't want your parents to experience the same grief as you. Sometimes, I would decide to do that every 24 hours for a great many days in a row.

[Two things in life change you, and you are never the same…

Love and Grief]

Thankfully, those days are a distant memory. Today, I was sitting all by myself and realized I had a smile on my face. I thought to myself, what's up with that? You're smiling. Then, I felt this warmth wash over me like the sun kissing my skin on a hot, sunny day. I felt a flutter in my tummy, a shiver of hope up and down my spine. I clutched my hands in a fist and held them close to my heart. I thought to myself, this feels peaceful; bask in these thoughts of knowing it's going to be okay. I will still have bad days, but I plan on focusing on the good ones. I got sticky notes and wrote on them, "I feel good about my life," to remind myself of that good feeling.

CJ looking at the ocean from the island of Unalaska.

The serenity prayer is from AA, and I would repeat that over and over. It was like a lifeline for me in my grief. Sometimes, I would say it without the hope of calming myself down. Other times, I would pay attention to the words and what it meant for me in that situation when I was praying: here's the serenity prayer, "God grant me the serenity to accept the things I cannot change, the courage to change the things I can, and the wisdom to know the difference."

"Keep it simple."

"One day at a time."

"Easy does it."

"Let go and let God."

"But for the grace of God."

"Live and let live."

These are more AA slogans I repeated to myself most days as needed. Sometimes, I would write them on sticky notes and plaster them everywhere. "Courage is not having the strength to go on. It's going on when you don't have the strength. "I also got that from AA. This rang true many days on my grief journey. I have a friend who sends me quotes that usually help me and are appropriate to my life at that moment.

I'm a big fan of quotes. Here's one, "and the moon said to me, my darling, you do not have to be whole in order to shine." After I lost CJ, I felt so broken. I felt like a part of me was missing. Another quote, "Believe in yourself. You are braver than you think and capable of more than you imagine." I repeated this many times until I could believe that I did not think I was capable of living without CJ.

"Don't let the entire staircase overwhelm you. Just focus on the first step." When I looked at things with that attitude, I could focus on the first step; it became more manageable and not so overwhelming, and then I could focus on the second step. I avoided looking up at the whole staircase. I knew it was there. I just kept telling myself one step at a time. With time, I worked my way up the entire flight of stairs.

"You're braver than you believe, stronger than you seem, and smarter than you think." The more you say these quotes of wisdom, the sooner you will begin to believe them for yourself. Say them out loud. Write them on sticky notes and plaster them everywhere in your house. When you walk, post the sticky notes, and say the quote several times, it will take time to believe what you are saying. It does not happen overnight. I had a friend who would tell me to drive my own bus. I would visualize my tricked-out hippie bus with me at the wheel door open, chasing people off my bus.

He also told me I needed to stay away from the hole. That when I found myself circling the hole, I needed to backtrack and think about something else, take a different path that leads away from the hole. I worked very hard to get out of that hole of grief. To this day, I find myself circling the hole.

I had so many journals. In one, I wrote letters to CJ. Some were angry letters, sad letters, and letters about my grief journey. No matter what I was feeling, I wrote them down. Another journal was for writing about what was happening that day and how it affected me. The third journal was my rambling when I was trying to control my thoughts. I didn't pay attention to the grammar, proper sentences, or even punctuation.

I didn't worry about neatness, and if I left any words out, I would write down the loudest thoughts. My thoughts would be racing around and around in my head, each one wanting the lead position. I wrote as quickly as I could. This would force my thoughts to slow down. Granted, the other thoughts would get impatient and want to be heard. Journaling helped me get my thoughts out of my head. Sometimes, I would go back and read what I wrote. There were times my writing was so bad that

I had no idea what I wrote, which was probably for the best. That meant it was out of my overworked head.

I had several people trying to help me find a grief group to join, but because of COVID, they were all shut down, so I joined online grief groups. Those helped me for a while. It was a place I could share how I was feeling, and someone would say yes, I felt, or I feel that same way. It helped me to know that I wasn't the only one who felt that way. The groups I was in mostly talked about their struggles. There weren't very many positive messages or words of hope. A few people were very judgmental. I shared that I made a memory showcase with my son's things and pictures that made me feel better. I could look at it and talk to CJ. A couple of people told me I had to take it down after the first year. I still have it set up in my living room three years later. I will always have a "CJ Showcase" set up in my house. As I worked through my grief, I realized these groups were bringing me down, so I decided to leave these groups from my phone. Luckily, I was attending "GriefShare," and I did not miss those groups, "but they served their purpose for a while.

I was given, and I bought a few books online about grief. One was "Grief Day by Day." I tried reading it, but I felt like it was too much to commit to, and I didn't attempt that book. I had another book on grief, which had input from a lot of grieving parents. It just seemed so overwhelming, and way too much info to focus on. That was my problem. I could not comprehend what I was reading. My mind would wander off as I was reading. I couldn't remember what I had read 10 minutes before.

When I started writing this book, I glanced over the grief books I had; there was some good information in them. In my opinion, keep going back to them. Keep trying to read them. They may help you in some way, which is my hope for you when you read my book. In hindsight, the grief books would have helped me some if I had kept going back and reading them until the information sunk into my grief, fogged brain.

[People think I have survived your leaving.

What they don't understand is that I have to relearn how to survive each day,

Because each day you are still gone...]

You will live with your grief for the rest of your life. It's a part of you now. You never get over your grief. It never completely goes away. You'll forever miss your lost loved one, but it does get easier. I read somewhere that it's like when you break a leg, it eventually heals, but now you walk with a limp, and on cold days it aches. There will always be sad days.

Now, it's how you deal with those sad days that matter. It's okay to circle the hole. Just don't fall into it. Take a step backward. It's okay to remember and have those feelings of grief. Just think about them as a memory and don't relive them. Always remember, it's okay to walk away from that hole and take another path. It's okay not to think about the lost one constantly. It's okay to feel better. It's okay to be happy again. It's okay to smile. It's okay to laugh. It's okay to enjoy life. It doesn't mean you forgot about them. It means you have learned to live without them. Most likely, your lost loved one wants you to live your life again, not just for you but for them as well. Go on adventures and take them with you.

For me I had to remember what happiness was, to learn to smile, to practice laughing, to figure out what would bring me joy. It wasn't easy but I didn't give up. The first time I had a day filled with fun and didn't think about CJ constantly I felt guilty. That night when I went back to my motel room, I cried myself to sleep.

Chapter 7

Keeping CJ Alive in My Heart

[A mother instinctively protects her child. A grieving mother instinctively protects her child's memory.

Author Unknown]

Even though CJ is gone from my sight, I keep him alive in my heart. I choose to believe that he is watching over me. He's my guardian angel. I talk to CJ every single day, several times throughout the day. I talk about CJ on a daily basis. I share my memories with others. I don't want to forget about them or him. I don't want anyone else to forget about him, either. I'm always saying, I'm sorry. I talk too much about CJ. The memories I share are all I have left, so I guess I'm not sorry, and I will talk about him forever. Another way to preserve the memories is to write them down and put them in a journal.

Late one night, I was agitated, sad, overwhelmed, and could not sleep, so I took a bubble bath with candles lit while listening to one of CJ's playlists I had created. I was sitting in the tub, ugly-crying, and wondering what CJ's spirit animal was. For my grandma, it was hummingbirds. I thought CJ loved all animals, but I did not know what his favorite animal was or even if he had one. This was very upsetting for me. That night I was consumed and extremely emotional with what CJ's spirit animal was. I was desperate for an answer.

I had my eyes closed trying to stop the tears as I cried out "CJ, I don't know what your spirit animal is. I don't know which animal to look for to make me think of you when I see it. I finally opened my eyes at looked down at the bubbles engulfing me. In front of me there was a patch of water with no bubbles I could see the water. It was in the perfect shape of a rabbit. I happily decided despite the tears that CJ's spirit animal was a rabbit and CJ himself answered my desperate plea.

When I first got CJ's stuff in the mail, I put the boxes in the spare bedroom in the closet.

We had the bedroom set up to be CJ's room. He was moving to Washington to be close to family. He told me it was a temporary thing that living with his mom and grandma would cramp his style. He wanted to go to college to study computers. He died a week before he was scheduled to move here. With CJ's stuff in the closet, I looked around the room, crying. I walked out and closed the door. It took me a couple of months to walk into that bedroom again. It was late at night, and I couldn't sleep, so I sat on the floor in front of the closet and opened my first box. Inside on top was one of CJ's quilts. I pulled it out, tears running down my cheeks; I helped it to my face and hugged the blanket tightly. I closed the box, not looking at anything else, and then went back to bed. I could smell CJ on the blanket. I wrapped myself in the blanket and cried myself to sleep.

[Small things can trigger a fresh wave of grief… A smell, a look, or perhaps a song…

Within seconds, you are flung into a time machine and are transported back to that 'moment' when time stood still and the world had crashed at your feet.

Zoe Clark-Coats]

In the boxes were CJ's clothes and personal items including his handkerchiefs. He always had a handkerchief in his pocket. My mom made me two memory blankets out of them. CJ wore a lot of dress shirts, my mom cut the pockets which snapped closed, and the sleeves with snaps on them and made a fidget blanket for me.

The memorial fidget blanket my mom made for me out of CJ's shirts and handkerchiefs.

She also made pillows out of some of his shirts. I gave those to who were close to CJ. I have a memorial showcase in my living room. I have photos of CJ in there, plus some of his childhood toys, his bible and sunglasses, his urn and the crystal vase with all the layers of sand plus cardinals that I have gotten in the past few years.

Every year at Christmas, I buy a new cardinal. I also have several memorial trinkets that I have ordered online. They have CJ's name on them, plus his birth and death year; there's a photo of a cardinal, a feather, an angel wings, or of CJ on the front with a short message. I have a memorial necklace, a key chain, plaques, and little ornaments. I have poems written on canvas and beautiful, thick paper. I have photos of CJ all throughout my house. Every photo holds a happy memory that I think about each time I look at them. I had photos of CJ put on wood to add a little variety to my memorial decor. I made a memorial journal with photos of CJ, notes from teachers, ribbons, sports certificates, his birth and death certificate, my marriage license to his father, and his school ID cards. It's full of mementos of CJ. A friend made me a beautiful scrapbook in beautiful, yellow-themed paper, with lots of pockets and foldouts that I filled with all of CJ's childhood pictures of different family members.

I try to go to CJ's memorial site in Montana I sit on the edge of the bank and toss rocks into the water and talk to CJ. His cross is still there, along with the painted rocks everyone brought which is so special to me. When I can, I camp at CJ's spot. I soak up the sun, breathed in the mountain air, put my feet in the water and recharge. The happy memories wash over me.

I got this deck of cards online. It is called "Talking to Heaven" mediumship cards by James Van Praagh. When I was struggling in the early days, I would sit in my room quietly with lit candles around me. I chose to believe that if I focused on CJ while holding the deck of cards against my heart, he would speak to me through the cards. The first number that popped into my head was how many times I shuffled the deck. The next number I thought of, I counted cards until I got to that number and then flipped the card over and read the message. I would do this and continue to draw cards. This gave me great comfort. I felt like CJ was guiding me on which card to pick to give me a special message. Here are a few cards that I drew quite often that provided me with the most comfort.

CJ told me (they read);

"I am standing right next to you."

"You have nothing to feel guilty about."

"I always give you a goodnight kiss."

"I watch over you every day."

"I send you loving signs through nature."

The last one I got the most. Ever since I lost CJ, I have found many heart-shaped rocks. I found two pinecones lying in a heart shape, and I found heart-shaped leaves. I was really struggling one day, and I found a pile of dog poop shaped like a heart. On the first anniversary of CJ's death, I went rock-hounding. I put the rocks I found in my rock tumbler, and out came a perfect little heart-shaped rock. On the second-year anniversary of CJ's death, I found a heart-shaped potato chip. I took pics of these hearts that I found only keeping the heart-shaped rocks. In a pile of trash, I found a beautiful crystal angel holding a heart that was only about two inches tall. I have that in CJ's showcase. I choose to believe CJ sent me these things, saying, "Mom, I love you, and here's something to remind you of my love for you."

Liz Newman]

I still write CJ letters. They are not so angry anymore. I tell him what's in my heart. I saved letters and cards I had gotten from CJ over the years. I sometimes pull a handful out of the box and reread them.

When I was going through CJ's stuff, I found a tattoo he designed on a scrap piece of paper. CJ had many tattoos. My favorite one he had was a barcode, and where the numbers were supposed to be, it read "Seige of Dark," which was located just below his belly button. The last one he designed has his initial CJK stacked on top of each other with the instructions on what color and shading he wanted in the margins. I have decided this year that I'm getting that tattoo, and just below his initials, I'm adding "Forever 33". This will be my very first tattoo.

Family and friends have gotten tattoos in honor of CJ and have sent me photos of them. I'm going to make a new scrapbook with all the photos of tattoos everyone has gotten in honor of him. Plus, all the photos I take on my adventures on CJ's anniversaries and birthdays.

I started a Facebook page for CJ. It's under CJ King, and it has a photo of CJ at the top; I encouraged friends and family to join. I posted photos of CJ and asked members to share their stories about CJ. I posted messages to CJ, and many shared grief quotes, which gave me great comfort. Others posted their photos of CJ. I got a lot of support, love, and encouraging words on CJ's page. It's still up and running. Today. I still post messages to CJ about my adventures in the anniversaries of his death. I keep it up for me. When I can't sleep at night, I like to scroll through the page and see how far I've come in my grief journey.

For a long time, I have been obsessed with CJ. He's all I could think about. I had regrets I had to accept. I thought, if only I had done this or that differently. I wish I had talked to him more; I would have written him more letters, hugged him a little longer the last time I saw him, and made more of an effort to try to see him. Today, my grief does not dominate my life. I do have a lot of memorial stuff for CJ, and his pictures are everywhere I talk about and talk to CJ daily. This keeps CJ alive for me. I have started going on adventures again, visiting and chatting with friends. I started crafting again. I started scrapbooking. It's much more advanced and popular than it was years ago. I'm thinking about selling my stuff online.

I mentioned this because scrapbooking brings me joy. I spend all my free time creating projects. I savor the good feelings I experience when crafting. I'm doing more of what brings me joy today. Thinking about CJ brings a smile to my face, followed by a happy thought and a warm feeling in my heart.

Chapter 8

CJ's Story

Always wanted to be a mom. I was very excited when I found out I was pregnant. I was 19 years old when I had CJ. We had a rocky start. CJ was born with pneumonia and spent ten days in the hospital. I started hemorrhaging and had to have my uterus scraped and received two units of blood. Since we were both sick, we didn't get to see each other for a few days. The nurses were great. One confessed to me that they were holding CJ all the time and that he rarely got put down.

CJ was a happy baby. He was so easygoing. He adapted to his environment. Whatever the situation. He loved going for rides in the car but hated being stuck in a car seat. From an early age, he would break out of his car seat. We must have gone through half a dozen or more car seats, which he all escaped out of. Just when I was running out of car seats and ideas, I got one he finally liked and accepted.

When CJ was about two and a half years old, I bought him some plastic boats to play with during bath time. He got it in his head that he was going to float his boats in the toilet. We ended up putting a flip latch lock on the bathroom door at the top to keep him out. Within a few hours, CJ had a stick horse; with the horse's head in his hands, he used the stick end to pop open the latch lock on the bathroom door, and he walked in all proud of himself.

CJ always had a great love for books. Before he could read, he loved being read too. My grandma had health issues, and some days, she was in bed a lot. CJ would ask, read me a book, grandma, and she would reply, I will read you two books to you. He would then bring as many books as he could carry to Grandma. They would lay in bed reading every book he had brought upstairs. They often fell asleep reading together.

When CJ was three and a half for almost a year, he wanted to be called Jack. Grandma would spend hours telling the grandkids nursery rhymes. CJ's favorite one was, "Jack be nimble, Jack be quick, Jack jumped over the candlestick." He decided one day, out of the blue, that he was Jack. On his fourth birthday, we threw a huge Batman birthday party for him. On the birthday banners and birthday cake, we put Happy Birthday Jack.

Once CJ learned to read, he spent a lot of his time reading. Every night at bedtime, he would read until he fell asleep. Some nights, I would have to tell him to put the book down and go to sleep. CJ would often reply, "I'm almost done with this chapter. Can I please finish it?"

He was in the third grade when he discovered the Goosebumps series. His teacher was very proud and impressed that he was reading those books. Well, one night, he was reading a Goosebumps book. I told him, "Lights out."

He had a flashlight, and he continued reading under the covers. I was in the bathroom, sitting on the washing machine, talking to CJ's stepdad as he was finishing up his shower. Unknown to us, CJ got scared reading his book, so he was standing just outside the bathroom door. About that time, my husband with a loud pop opened a can of beer. CJ screamed like a girl loudly and flew into the bathroom, wrapping his arms around my legs.

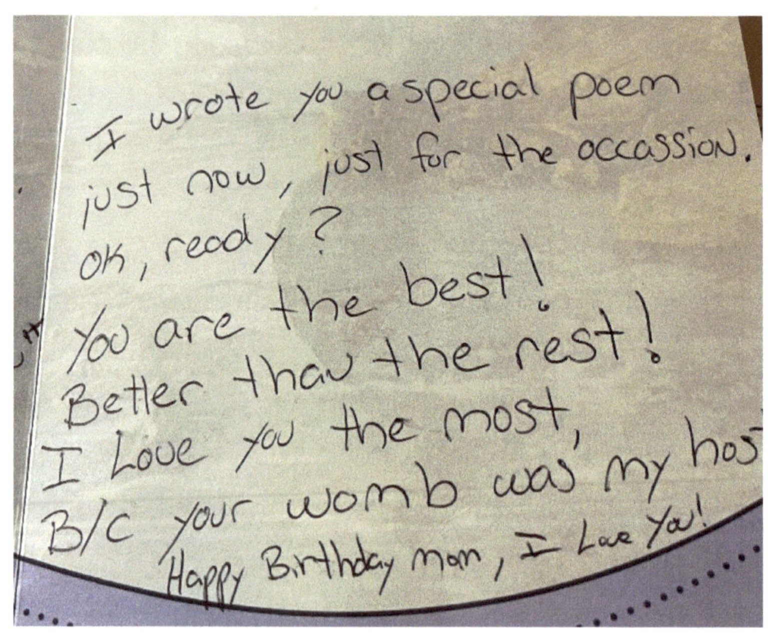

A birthday poem from CJ

A Mother's Day poem from CJ

CJ also wrote stories and poems. A lot of his stories were dark that had a deep meaning. He was always writing a short poem in my cards and letters. I wish I had more of his writings, I have a few I cherish greatly. CJ was also a talented artist. I often wish he would have spent more time drawing. He mostly drew on scrap pieces of paper. He would often draw pics on the envelopes he sent me.

Artwork **CJ** did on envelopes.

I loved you your whole life,

I will miss you the rest of mine]

CJ has always loved me more than anybody else. I've said that a lot over the last three years. I asked myself, what makes you think that? Why do you believe that? For starters, after CJ passed away, several of CJ's friends reached out to me, and one of the first things they usually said was, CJ loved you the most. He talked about you all the time. When he needed to make several calls, you were the first one he called. In the early days of my grief, I felt guilty for some of the things I did that affected CJ.

I made some mistakes. As a mother, CJ never blamed me for those mistakes, even when they affected him badly. Another thing everyone said to me was that CJ never spoke a harsh word against you or blamed you for anything. He always said you did the best you could and that you were the best mom ever. CJ always made sure I knew he loved me. Every time we talked, he told me how much he loved me, even from an early age. He would give me notes or send me letters and cards, postcards, and text messages saying he was thinking about me and that he loved me. CJ was very good about sending me messages when I was struggling, saying that it would get better. That better days are coming.

CJ was my biggest cheerleader. He was so proud of me for going to college when I was in my forties. He was just as excited as I was when I got my diploma. He said I encouraged him by going to college, that he took night classes, and that he got his GED. He scored in the top 3%. I got straight A's. We bragged to each other about our accomplishments. I was so proud of CJ for getting his GED, which I told him many times.

CJ always had a smile and a hug to give you. He gave the best hugs. Maybe that's because he put so much love into those hugs. I will forever miss those hugs and the smiles that went with them. I heard so many stories about how CJ helped them during a low point in their lives that he cheered them on. He was a shoulder for them to cry on. He would quietly build them up until they could believe in themselves and their capabilities.

CJ had a great sense of humor. He loved telling jokes. Whenever he was young, I bought him several joke books. There were moments when I wanted to throw those books on the wood stove. CJ carried them around everywhere, reading jokes out loud to anyone who would listen. Even if that meant following you around the house, CJ would tell a joke, and then he'd laugh the loudest. I just want to see CJ for a short time make up the dumbest jokes; what I wouldn't give today to have my fair-haired, blue-eyed, sweet little boy following me around and telling me one joke after another.

When CJ was four years old, he had a faded Levi jacket and a pair of gray snakeskin cowboy boots.

CJ in his favorite Levi jacket and cowboy boots

They were by far his favorite and had to be worn always. He tried to wiggle his body into them long after he outgrew them. I'm not what happened to the jacket or boots. At the age of 10, he had a favorite T-shirt with a with a band on it that he loved. As the shirt started to fall apart, he would put it back together with safety pins. When we finally threw it away, it had close to 30 safety pens piecing the shirt together.

One of my grandma's favorite stories about CJ was when he was almost three years old. His favorite color was pink, so I had gotten him a pink bucket for Easter. He either wore that bucket on his head or he carried it around full of toys. One morning, he was downstairs in his toy room playing. As we were putting the toys away, I discovered pee in the beloved pink bucket. I was mortified. I looked at CJ and asked why. He said it was too far to the bathroom, and he didn't want to stop playing. The bathroom was almost straight across the hallway from the toy room. I slightly overreacted and threw the bucket into the trash. He never let me forget about throwing his beloved pink bucket away. My grandma said I could have bleached it out, but I was not going to let him put it on his head after he peed in it.

CJ also had to grow up with a mom who was a neat freak. I felt everything had a place, and when it was not in use, it had to be in its proper place. Every single night before bed and often throughout the day, CJ and I would organize and properly put his toys away. One basket was for cars, one for blocks, one for ninja turtles, one for army men, and one for little plastic animals. The books were organized on the bookshelves. Shirts hanging up. Pants, shorts, socks, and undies each had their own drawers. His shoes lined up neatly in the closet. His bed was made. He would joke with me and say, "Mom, you taught me how to be organized." He was a neat freak, too.

CJ was an active boy. He went all in, no matter what he was doing. When he was in kindergarten, just before Christmas break, he was at school playing on this 25-foot slide, waiting his turn to go down. It was snowing and icy out, he lost his footing and fell from the slide from the top. Luckily, he was wearing a snowsuit and fell onto a pile of snow. Unfortunately, there was a rock, and he hit the side of his head on it. He ended up with a black eye that covered half his face.

Later that year, just before spring break, CJ was out at recess playing catch with a hard baseball. When a classmate yelled his name, he turned his head to look just as the ball was thrown his way. He got hit in the side of his head, close to his temple. I'm seven months pregnant. As I waddled my way into the school, the first person I saw was the janitor. He smiled and winked at me and said he pissed me off, so I hit him. A little concerned, I tried to hurry down the hall. The principal caught me before I could walk into the nurse's office; he shook his head and said, it looks worse than it really is. He continues with; I must say that if this accident and the one at Christmas had not happened at school, we would have called child services on you. Not going to lie; I panicked. I brushed past him and went rushing into the nurse's office. Here's CJ with an ice pack on his head, talking to the nurse. As I walk in, he looks at me and smiles, and says, "Hi, Mom."

Then, when he was in the fifth grade, he went skiing with the school. On his second skiing trip, he fell, and with the ski pole still clutched in his hand, he fell on it, breaking his thumb. Later that spring, he was swinging on the swing at school, and while he was high in the air, he jumped out and broke his wrist. On that same hand as the broken thumb. To put it nicely, CJ would test his boundaries and see how far he could go. He was always up for a new adventure. He usually got caught quickly. Sometimes, I think that kid had the worst luck.

He was in the fourth grade when he started a gang at school. During recess, two groups of kids would go out behind this brick wall, and they would wrestle in the dirt. Nobody got hurt, and it was shut down very quickly. But that story followed CJ all throughout school. When he started junior high, CJ's English teacher told me at the end of the first quarter during a conference that she dreaded having CJ as a student because of the gang business. But to her surprise and much delight, CJ was one of her favorite students. She told me she could give him a word, and he could come up with a synonym word for her.

CJ's junior high math teacher said he could do a word math problem and come up with another formula for solving it than what she had. She could use the formula to solve other word problems and it would work for them too. She tried putting CJ in advanced math class, but they had homework every night and CJ refused to do it, so he asked me to take him out of it.

When CJ was in the 7th grade, they got computers in the school. CJ would come home from school and say, I got pulled out of class to help with the computers. I'm not sure how it all came about, but CJ helped the teacher set up and work out some of the kinks with the computers. I was so proud of him for doing that. He had his hands full when we got our first computer at home. He set up our computer and taught me how to use it. Many times, saying I will show you how one more time, only to do it 20 more times.

I could fill pages and pages with treasured memories I have of CJ. I will end this chapter with one of my favorite stories. At first, CJ wanted this story kept quiet, but later on, he joined in on the humor of it. When CJ was ten years old, he was taking a shower. We had a dark curtain for the shower. We only had one bathroom, so quite often, your privacy was invaded. I went into the bathroom to pull some clothes out of the dryer. I smelled smoke. I'm thinking, what's going on? I look around and see smoke coming from the top of the shower curtain. As

I flung open the shower curtain, I said, "What the hell are you doing?" CJ has a horrified look on his face. He didn't know what to do with his hands, whether to hide his cigarette or cover his privates. I'm standing there looking at him, shocked. Finally, he says, "Mom, please, can I have some privacy?"

[You can shed tears because they are gone, or you can smile because they lived.

You can close your eyes and pray they will come back, or you can open your eyes and see all that they left for you. Your heart can be empty because you can't see them, or you can be full of the love you shared. You can turn your back on tomorrow and live for yesterday, or you can be happy for tomorrow because of yesterday. You can remember only that they are gone, or you can cherish their memory and let it live on. You can cry and close your mind and feel empty, or you can do what they would want. Smile, open your heart… and go on.

Elizabeth Ammons]

Chapter 9

Celebrating CJ's Life

[It's hard to turn the page when you know someone
won't be in next chapter,

But the story must go on…

Thomas Wilder]

The first birthday for CJ was less than two months after
he died. I stayed in bed most of the day crying. Mom went
and got balloons. We wrote messages on them, and we each
released three balloons into the sky in our backyard. I then
barbecued steaks for dinner. Right after dinner, I went back to
bed. That started the birthday tradition of releasing balloons
and BBQing steaks. Each year, it got a little bit easier to get
through the day. This year I celebrated CJ's birthday with balloons and steaks. Instead of spending the day in bed, Mom and
I went rock-hounding along the Puget Sound. It was another
day to honor CJ by going on an adventure and celebrating his
life. I also found a green heart-shaped rock to add to my col-
lection.

I go on adventures every year on the anniversary of CJ's
death. In my first year, I went rock-hounding with a friend.
We had lunch, and then we walked around a huge secondhand
store. I found a Fenton glass shoe to add to my showcase full
of them. I ran the rocks we found through my rock Tumbler,

and one of the rocks I pulled out of the batch was less than half an inch in size. It was a perfect, tiny heart shape. Milky white with brown specks. The second year, I went with another friend on my first ferry ride from Bremerton, Washington, to Seattle, Washington. Then back to Bremerton. I had seen the 720 and 520 floating bridges when I was flying into the Seattle Airport. I wanted to go across them, which I got to do that day. Later that day, I went to a secondhand store and found another Fenton shoe for my showcase and went out to dinner with Mom. This last year, my plans kept changing. A last-minute decision, Mom and I went to Snoqualmie Falls. We stopped at a couple of secondhand stores. This year, I found several Fenton shoes for my showcase. On our way home, we grabbed dinner. I take pictures to remember the day. I still have moments of sadness, but the emotions are not as intense as they once were, but they are new adventures I go on in honor of CJ and his life.

The one thing we talked about at length was how CJ wanted to be near family during the holidays. We even threw around ideas on what to do for our first holiday back together; the first holiday season after CJ was gone, I spent a lot of the time crying in bed. This last year, I went to Kansas and spent Christmas with my two grandbabies on their Christmas break. On Christmas day, I had a quiet moment, shed a few tears, and talked to CJ. Holidays will always be hard, but now I can enjoy the good despite the sadness. It's not like I can go buy CJ a shirt or give him a picture of his niece and nephew for Christmas or his birthday, so I buy Memorial trinkets for CJ and display them. It gives me joy to get them in the mail and then find a special spot for them.

My first Mother's Day without CJ was heartbreaking. I spent the day in bed crying. The second Mother's Day, I learned about the bereaved Mother's Day. It's the first Sunday in May, and it honors mothers who lost a child. It's also for mothers who cannot be a mother due to infertility or other health reasons. It's not a day we celebrate but a day we recognize. That the hole in our hearts is the worst. Here are a few short quotes about the grief of a mother:

"Your life was a blessing. Your memory, a treasure".

"The world changes from year to year and lives from day to day, but the love and memory of you shall never pass away."

"There are no goodbyes for us. Wherever you are, you'll always be in my heart".

"When someone you love becomes a memory, that memory becomes a treasure."

"If I had a flower for every time I thought of you, I would walk in my own garden forever."

"A mom hug lasts long after she lets go."

Unfortunately, no one will love your lost child as much as you do, but how could they? This is a holiday that many do not acknowledge, nor do they know what to say or to do for you on this day, so they do nothing. Then there are those who do not even know this is a special day. I am blessed! My mom always acknowledges this day by taking me out for lunch and buying me flowers.

In May of 2023, I got to go to Austin, Texas, and visit the area where CJ became my guardian angel. I went with my brother he's the one who got CJ's stuff, talked to the investigating officer and walked around the area he was found when it first happened. It was emotional as we approached the city.

CJ had expressed many times he wanted me to visit him in Texas and I never did. We went to CJ's old house, and I could see his bedroom window from the street. We drove around the neighborhood, and I thought about CJ walking those sidewalks and speeding on his bicycle down the streets.

The location where CJ's body was found is no longer available to go visit as it is now a college. After some searching, we found the area that changed my life forever. I was not able to leave flowers or some of his ashes. I'm thankful I got to go to Austin and walk the streets my son last walked. It provided me with much healing.

There are many ways to celebrate your lost loved one's memories. Besides what I've done, the things that have helped me. I have a friend who lights a white candle on CJ's death anniversary in remembrance of him.

You could also do some of these in remembrance:

Plant a tree, watching it grow, and letting it be a place to go for comfort in future anniversaries is another way.

Donate money in the memory of your lost loved one to a charity they may have supported, or one they thought was important.

You could take flowers to your lost loved one's memorial site, or to their grave site, or send flowers to a hospice or a nursing home, and write on the card in loving memory and sign their name.

Gather with friends and family to honor your loved one. Meet at a restaurant for dinner. Host a picnic or barbecue. Plan an activity to do together. Talk about the lost loved one. Share memories.

Create a memory box put snapshots, letters from your lost loved one and letters to them. Write down memories on pretty paper. Write down inspirational quotes and poems. Add mementos that remind you of them, and then on their anniversary or birthday, whatever day you choose, open the box and enjoy the beautiful memories.

Plan a quiet day of reflection. Take the day off from work. Spend time outside. Look at photos. Take a walk down memory lane. Turn your phone off. Take a nap. Go for a run or a hike.

All of which can be done in loving memory of your lost loved one.

We have CJ's memorial bench in our backyard with lots of pretty flowers planted all around. We sit on the bench and talk to CJ.

I also listen to music in remembrance of CJ. I put a post on Facebook and asked everyone if they had a song that made them think of CJ and why. I then created a playlist, adding those songs plus songs that made me think about CJ. Ones he sang loudly to when he heard them, or ones he danced around to. Songs that I remember him loving as he was growing up. Plus, there are a few songs about lost loved ones that I honor CJ with. One is "Dancing in the Sky" by Danna and Lizzie, "Scars in Heaven" by Casting Crowns, and "A Brighter Side of Grey" by Five Finger Death Punch. Another one I recently discovered is "When I Look to the Sky" by Train. I even remember singing a few gospel songs in church with my grandma.

[They say there is a reason

They say there is a reason; they say that time will heal.

But neither time nor reason will change the way I feel.

For no one knows the heartache, that lies behind our smiles.

No one knows how many times we have broken down and cried,

We want to tell you something so there won't be any doubt.

You're so wonderful to think of but so hard to be without.

Author Unknown]

Chapter 10

Time to Start Your Healing Journey

[My mind still talks to you. My heart still looks for you.

But my soul knows you are at peace.

Still Moments]

Start journaling immediately. The sooner, the better. Don't worry about what you are writing. Just write what's in your head and heart, even if it's a rambling bunch of incoherent thoughts. It does help to get those thoughts and feelings out of your head and on paper. It helps put them in perspective. It's an easy way to express, explore, and reflect on your feelings without judgment. Let's you vent without scrutiny. Journaling allows you to go back and read your past thoughts and feelings to see your progress. It's a record of your memories of your lost loved one. It helps calm your fears and your racing thoughts. It's not important what you write. Getting those thoughts and feelings out is what's important. Don't worry about punctuation, spelling, proper sentences, or even neatness. Untangling your thoughts and emotions is the beginning of healing in your grief journey.

Here are three different versions of grief. You will notice some stages are the same.

There are five stages of grief:

1. Denial – the period of grieving in which a person refuses to accept the reality of the loss. It's a defense mechanism that helps us protect ourselves from the shock of death. This is normal and helpful during the grieving process.

2. Anger – once you begin to comprehend the news of the death and start to accept the reality of the loss, you will experience anger. You can feel anger toward a person, place, event, situation, or even a lost loved one.

3. Bargaining – during grief, we often feel helpless and overwhelmed. A person will often negotiate or make compromises to get the lost loved one back. We often think, what if I did this or that? What if I was there more? Bargaining is often irrational.

4. Depression – a feeling of sadness and hopelessness as a result of the loss of your loved one. Some of the first stages of grief protect you from the emotional pain due to loss. These feelings are unavoidable and must be felt in order to work through your grief. Sometimes, it takes outside help to deal with your depression.

5. Acceptance – is when you finally come to terms with accepting the reality of your loss. We no longer deny or struggle against our grief. We instead work toward celebrating the life of our lost loved one, cherish the memories we shared, and then work toward moving forward.

There are also seven stages of grief:

1. Shock – Happens with almost every situation even if you had time to prepare for the death. We know it will happen, but you don't know the exact moment. People in shock will appear to be behaving normally without much emotion because the news hasn't fully sunk in. There's a feeling of numbness and a self-protective detachment from their feelings because it's too much to deal with all at once.

2. Denial – Many people experience denial after a death, they know something has happened, but it doesn't feel real.

3. Anger – Anger is a difficult emotion to deal with and can be minimized by others. We often hide this stage from others.

4. Bargaining – is about making promises to yourself or a higher being, asking the universe for a chance to put things right. You may seek reason where there is none, and may feel guilty about how you behaved, or feel in some way to blame.

5. Depression – The jumble of emotions that happens during the grieving process can lead to feelings of depression, isolation, anxiety, and a feeling of dread. Sometimes, it is too much to bear.

6. Acceptance and hope – acceptance is about realizing you can't change what happened, and then understanding you can control how you respond. Hope is knowing you can go on and move forward.

7. Processing grief – Everyone grieves differently. There's

no right or wrong way to grieve. There's no time limit to your grief, or a quick fix to get over grief.

There is another version of the seven stages of grief:

1. Shock – numbed disbelief toward the loss. It helps the feelings of loss from being so overwhelming.

2. Denial – The death of a loved one can have a significant impact on you, you will experience denial. At this stage, it's too hard for your brain to comprehend that your loved one is gone.

3. Anger – Your anger could be directed at a person, place, or event. Most often, you don't even know why you are angry; you just are. This replaces shock and denial. The numbness has disappeared.

4. Bargaining – is making promises and asking for things to go back to the way they were before you lost your loved one. Thinking maybe I could have done things differently.

5. Depression – You feel emptiness inside, lost, and alone. You experience great sadness. You withdraw from people and activities.

6. Testing – testing is the process of trying to find solutions that help you deal with the loss. You will often experience the other stages while going through this stage.

7. Acceptance – In this stage, you don't automatically get over the loss or stop feeling sad. It means you have accepted the loss. That you realize your life will never go back to the way it was before.

I struggled with every stage of grief listed above. My grief journey did not follow the order of the stages. Plus, I bounced around and would go back to a stage after I thought I was over it. I still struggle at times with anger, resentment, and sadness. But it's not as intense as it was in the beginning. When I experience sadness now, I self-talk my way through it. I will experience sadness on certain days of significance, or a memory, or a song, sometimes something on TV will set it off, or a comment made by someone in passing. I allow myself to feel the sadness but tell myself I can be sad for a certain amount of time. I give myself a deadline and figure out what triggered the sadness. I usually tell myself, "You can be sad until the sun rises tomorrow. Go ahead and feel the sadness. Let the sadness out. I am sad because today is Bereaved Mother's Day (or whatever the reason). It's okay. That made me sad. I will forever have sad days, but what I do with the sadness and how long it lasts is what I can control." It takes time to accomplish this, and many times, I would wake up and say I'm still sad, and then I would give myself to the next morning to be sad. I did that every morning until it worked. Be gentle with yourself when the sadness persists. I embrace the sadness, write a letter to CJ, look at photos and old letters, listen to meaningful music, watch movies CJ loved, and share memories of CJ. Don't stuff the sadness inside; it will surface in unwanted ways and usually occur at the wrong time.

[It's hard when you miss people. But you know, if you miss them, it means you were lucky.

It means you had someone special in your life, someone worth missing.

Kelly's Treehouse]

Once in a while, resentment will show their ugly face. I acknowledge the resentment and figure out what caused it to come back. Then, I remind myself that nobody is perfect. That the person did the best they could in that situation. Everyone has struggles that they don't talk about. I remind myself that nobody loves my son as much as I do. They have their own families, and we have drifted apart. I remind myself that forgiving that person helps me the most. By forgiving, I can let the resentment go. It's taking up valuable space in my brain. It doesn't mean I will forget I'm moving on.

Anger was the hardest for me to understand and control. For a long time, I didn't know how to get my anger out. I stuffed the anger until I exploded and lashed out at people and objects. I learned to control my anger by screaming into my pillow or while I was alone in my car, and when I was somewhere, nobody could hear me. Then, when the anger was out, or I was too hoarse to scream anymore, I began to focus on my breathing. I take deep, slow breaths in my nose and then let it out through my mouth. Imagine a peaceful scene with a waterfall or a stream of water. I also clench and then relax every muscle in my body until the tension is gone.

Here are some more ideas on how to get your anger out safely:

1. Throw or break something. Physically throw something like a rock, a ball, or a dish. Throw rolled-up socks or toilet paper at the wall or a target.

2. Dance it out. Dance to angry music and happy pump-you-up music.

3. Sing it out. Play music that expresses anger.

4. Do an intense workout. Go for a run, or do high impact aerobics, or weightlifting, or go on a hike up a steep trail or mountain.

5. Journal. Write as fast as you can; get those thoughts and feelings out.

6. Draw or paint. Be creative. Do a craft, make something.

7. Destroy a physical representation of your anger. Print an upsetting message, then scribble on it or tear it up.

8. Verbalize your anger to a friend, an object, or whatever to get it out. Yell, cuss, scream.

9. Change your surroundings. Go into another room, go outside. Disrupt your train of thought. Do a timeout.

Your grief journey will, most likely, be the hardest thing you ever do. At least it was for me. You may need help to work through the healing process. I needed antidepressants and mood stabilizers. I also stayed in the hospital twice. I talked to a counselor for over two years. I also joined grief groups. I discovered I could not heal myself without professional help. And that's okay; that's what the professionals are for. Remember to be gentle with yourself. If you struggle with finding help, ask someone to help you. If they don't know how to help you, keep asking until you get help. Ask a friend, family member, doctor, counselor, preacher, teacher, co-worker, neighbor, national hotline, google it, or even a stranger on the street. Please don't give up; you are worthy of help and healing. Unfortunately, when you call a national hotline, you will not be greeted immediately by a live person. Be patient, and you will be guided in the right direction. Hang in there, if not for yourself, then for your lost loved one.

[Grief is a very long journey, a journey you take on your own.

And no one can know all the sorrow you feel, for it's your sorrow alone.

Grief is an awful intruder; it comes and stays night and day.

And no one can look at the way you grieve and then tell you

No, this is the way.

Anne Peterson]

You will grieve and mourn for your lost loved one for a very long time. Here are the 6 R's of mourning:

1. Recognize - the loss. First, you must experience the loss and understand that it has happened.

2. React – you will react emotionally to the loss.

3. Recollect & re-experience – you may review memories of your lost loved one. (Events that occurred, places visited together, or day-to-day moments that were experienced together).

4. Relinquish – you begin to put the loss behind you. Realizing and accepting that the world has truly changed and that there is no turning back.

5. Re-adjust – you begin the process of returning to daily life, and the loss starts to feel less acute and sharp.

6. Reinvest – Ultimately you re-enter into the world, forming new relationships and commitments. You accept the changes that have occurred and move past them.

Then there's the 3 Cs of grief:

1. Choose – As you go through your grief journey, you choose what is best for you. It's normal to feel a loss of control when you lose a loved one. You feel like you need to accept the world around you and that you have no say. It may be hard to do the day-to-day activities, but you always have a choice. You may experience brain fog, which is when your brain feels muddled and cloudy, and you can't think clearly. Find someone who has your best interest at heart and ask them for help. You then can decide whether to do it or not.

2. Connect – Grief is very isolating and great feelings of loneliness. It's very important to connect with others even if you are normally a loner, it's important for your mind and well-being. We are not meant to do this life alone. Nobody can fix your grief, but having someone close by is comforting.

3. Communicate – By communicating to your friends and family about your needs and what works best for you in any given situation allows them to productively help you. So, when you are struggling, they can help you begin to heal. The worst thing to do is isolate, pretend to be okay or downplay your grief.

We all deal with grief differently. There's no wrong way to deal with it except when we stuff our feelings or numb the grief with alcohol and/or drugs.

Here are some ways to honor and memorialize a loved one:

1. Personalize a photo. Whether it be painted or done on canvas, wood, tile, or glass.

2. Organize a fundraiser event in their name. Donate money, time, or material items in their name.

3. Create a playlist. Songs your lost loved one liked, songs that remind you of them, songs that honor them now that they are gone.

4. Write a song or poem about your loved one. Create a journal with stories about them.

5. Name a business or item about them. Create something new and attach their name to it.

6. Make a photo calendar collage or a multi-slot photo frame.

7. Share a favorite recipe of theirs, and cook their favorite meal to share.

8. 8.Always pray for them.

9. Fly a kite, release balloons, and light luminary balloons.

10. Light a candle in remembrance.

11. Buy memorial trinkets and ornaments with their name, a picture, birth and death dates, and a special quote.

12. Create a memorial scrapbook. Put photos, letters and cards they wrote, birth and death certificate, awards and honors they got, their artwork, poems and stories. Anything that brings back a memory of them.

13. Create a memorial website. I started one on Facebook for family and friends to post photos and memories of my son. Many posted inspirational quotes.

14. Get a tattoo. Many of CJ's family and friends have gotten tattoos to honor him.

15. Memorial jewelry with their photo, name, birth, and death date, and a special poem or quote. I have a memorial necklace that has some of CJ's ashes in it.

16. Frame their correspondence or artwork, a story or poem they wrote. Some of their childhood schoolwork.

17. Finish one of their projects or ideas. For instance, I'm getting a tattoo CJ designed for himself but never got a chance to get done.

18. Plant a tree or memorial garden. That way, you can go back and visit and watch the fruits of your labor grow.

19. Adopt a loved one's hobby or goal or continue their work on a favorite charity or cause.

20. Have a BBQ, picnic, or gathering in your lost loved one's honor. Have everyone share stories.

21. Start a tradition in your loved one's honor, whether it be making a special or favorite meal for dinner on their birthday. Go on a hike or camping, something you can do on a regular basis.

22. Take some of their ashes and put them in the ink for a tattoo or in a piece of blown glass. Release some of their ashes at a special location.

23. Make a documentary. Video family, friends, co-work-

ers, and neighbors while you interview them. Compile a video of mini videos and photos of your loved one.

24. Have a movie or game night in their honor. Play games or watch movies they like.

25. Write them letters, journal about them. Then, you can go back and reread what you wrote and see how far you've come on your grief journey.

26. Adopt a park, a landmark or star in your lost loved one's name. Install a memorial bench, sponsor maintenance in a park or along the road in their honor.

27. Publish a memorial tribute in the newspaper or magazine, whether it be an obituary, a memorial service, or a story about them. Or write a book about them like I have.

28. Take a trip to places your lost loved one enjoyed going to, places you went together, or places you both wanted to go. Even carry out things on their bucket list.

29. Start something new in their honor. Start a new tradition or continue one they loved.

30. Create a memorial in your loved one's honor. It could be a memorial showcase or bookcase. Put a cross at the spot where they died. I created a memorial with a cross that has CJ's name on it, and painted rocks were brought to his memorial service and placed all around the ground surrounding the cross. It was placed at one of our favorite swimming holes. We also have a memorial bench in our yard with flowers planted all around it and memorial plaques.

[Dearest CJ, you are finally home with me. Not the way I wanted.

I laid in bed last night and held your ashes; I was wrapped in your blanket on your pillow and cried myself to sleep.

Tonight, I made your memorial showcase. I feel a little peace tonight I miss you so very much. I love you more than you could imagine.

I'm so sorry you didn't get to have a baby of your own or find your soulmate. I wish you had more happiness. You brought me so much happiness and joy.

Love, Mommy]

31. Get a jar, book, or even poster board. Have everyone write a quote or special phrase on small pieces of paper and fill it out instead of just names in a guest book. I created a jar of sand with layers of different colors of sand representing every story told at CJ's memorial.

Here are a few ideas for coping with your grief:

1. Connect with others. A friend, a family member, a medical professional, a support group or even a priest.

2. Ask for help in whatever form is needed.

3. Practice deep breathing regularly.

4. Set small, realistic goals.

5. Ensure you are getting enough sleep and aim for some form of movement each day.

6. Eat a healthy, balanced diet and keep hydrated.

7. Rehearse how to respond to questions and new situations.

8. Develop a daily routine. Focus on things you can control.

9. Celebrate the life of your lost loved one.

10. Work on finding joy. Experiencing joy can help improve your mental state.

11. Learn about different ways to process grief.

12. Binge-watch TV series or movies you've already seen. I could not focus for long on anything, and the TV was a good distraction. My mind would wander, and then I would go back to the TV. I didn't have to rewind it since I had already seen what I missed before.

Here are some things not to do during your grief journey:

1. Avoid your pain and refuse to allow yourself to grieve.

2. Live in the past

3. Idolize the lost loved one.

4. Refuse to make the necessary changes to move forward.

5. Dwell in self-pity. But allow yourself to feel the pain while also making efforts to take healthy steps toward healing.

6. Lose respect for own body. Don't neglect your physical needs.

7. Remain withdrawn or run away from your feelings.

8. Rely on alcohol and/or drugs.

9. Maintain unrealistic expectations of what others should offer in comfort.

10. Resent others with intact families.

11. Expect yourself to get over it. You never completely will.

12. Guilt over good days. It's okay to be happy.

13. Crossing bridges before you get to them instead of taking it one day at a time.

14. Condemn yourself.

15. Underestimate yourself. You will be okay.

16. Get involved in a serious relationship before you have worked through the stages of grief.

17. Make any major changes or decisions if you can help with them.

Take pictures of everything and everyone. Don't care about who you annoy by constantly taking pictures. In the end, they will be all you have left. Every photo is a memory – capture it…

Writing this book has been an amazing healing experience for me. I want to thank you for taking the time to read about my grief journey. I truly hope I have helped you in some way. There's a saying it takes a village to raise a child. It takes a great support system to recover from the loss of a child. It should not be done on your own. Just know that there is a light at the end of the tunnel, so keep moving forward blindly. You will make it. Nobody grieves the same way because your relationship with your lost loved one is unique and special. Remember to be gentle with yourself and know that your lost loved one will always be alive in your heart. I'm sending you healing and positive energy.

One of the last pics of CJ

I would like to say a special Thank you to Annie McIndoo for sharing her writing program, which allowed me to heal and honor my son. In the span of ten months, this idea was turned into an extraordinary experience that resulted in a heartfelt story about love and loss.

References

Grief Share:

https://www.griefshare.org

National Mental Health Hotline:

866-903-3787

https://mentalhealthhotline.org

Call or text:

988 or,

Chat: 988lifeline.org

Crisis Text Line:

Text Home to 741-741

For free 24/7

https://www.crisistextline.org

Mental Health Helpline. International Directory:

https://www.helpguide.org

1-800-950-6264

Or text: Nami to 741-741

Substance Abuse and Mental Health Services Administration:

800-662-4357

Veterans Crisis Line:

Call 988, Then Press 1

Text: 838-255

Grief Books I Have:

Shattered

Surviving the loss of a child

By: Gary Roe

Grief Day by Day

Simple Practices and Daily Guidance for Living with Loss

By: Jan Warner

A Time to Mourn, A Time to Dance

Helps for the Losses in Life

Provided by: Thrivent Financial – Connecting Faith and Finances for Good

Grief Share – Workbook

Your Journey from Mourning to Joy

www.griefshare.org

Writing to Heal the Soul

Transforming Grief and Love Through Writing

By: Susan Zimmermann

The 12 Stages of Healing

A Network Approach to Wholeness

By: Donald M. Epstein D.C.

Founder & Developer of Network Chiropractic

With Nathaniel Altman